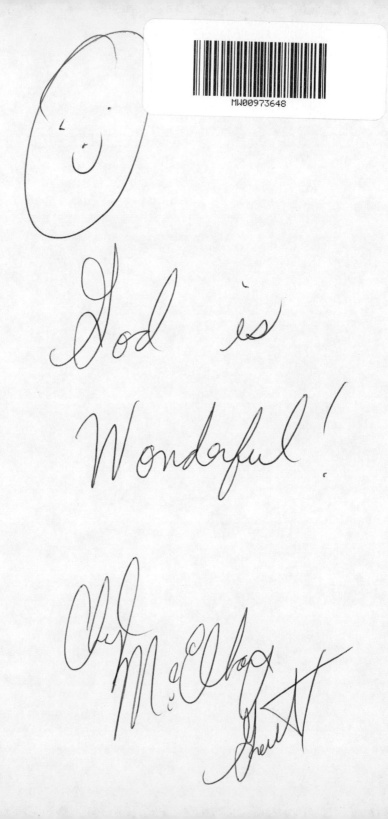

God is

Wonderful!

Your Life Can Change
in 1 Minute

Cheryl McElhaney Garrett

WestBow
PRESS
A DIVISION OF THOMAS NELSON

WestBow Press books may be ordered through booksellers or by contacting:

WestBow Press
A Division of Thomas Nelson
1663 Liberty Drive
Bloomington, IN 47403
www.westbowpress.com
1-(866) 928-1240

Because of the dynamic nature of the Internet, any web addresses or links contained in this book may have changed since publication and may no longer be valid. The views expressed in this work are solely those of the author and do not necessarily reflect the views of the publisher, and the publisher hereby disclaims any responsibility for them.

ISBN: 978-1-4497-4149-5 (sc)
ISBN: 978-1-4497-4148-8 (hc)
ISBN: 978-1-4497-4150-1 (e)

Library of Congress Control Number: 2012903205

Any people depicted in stock imagery provided by Thinkstock are models, and such images are being used for illustrative purposes only.

Certain stock imagery © Thinkstock.

Printed in the United States of America

WestBow Press rev. date: 2/22/2012

Author's Note:
All Doctors' names have been changed.

Contents

Chapter 1

Why?

I opened one eye and could see only shadows. I opened my other eye and saw my family standing around me. I tried to speak, but only a coarse voice came out of my throat. I asked, "Where am I?"

My mother answered slowly. "You are in a hospital."

My mind started racing and the first thing I thought of was: *Why?* My body felt like I had been in a car wreck. It ached and tingled all over. I tried to raise my body, but there was like a force holding me down. Then my eyes connected with my mother's and I saw sadness in her eyes. I was so anxious to learn why she had that expression. I kept asking, "Why? Why?"

She came close to me and whispered, "You have spinal bacterial meningitis for the second time in fourteen months."

I had disbelief in my mind. I am forty-nine years old and had it twice in my life. I felt like I had become a burden to my family and friends. I didn't want to go through the pain and suffering that was inflicted on everyone last year. I felt that me not being here on earth anymore would make everyone's life easier. I felt like I wanted to go away, and I went into a coma. I found out your life can change in one minute.

Chapter 2

Monday, Monday, Monday Morning

My feet hit the bedroom floor very softly. I had just said my morning prayer, which I did ever morning when I got up, and done my regular routine for the morning. I walked my dog, straightened up the house, woke up my daughter Faith, and got us ready for work and school. It seemed like a typical Monday morning in Corryton, TN where I live, but little did I know that the day would end at the hospital for the first time with spinal bacterial meningitis.

I arrived at work around 7:15 a.m. and everything was normal until 10:00 a.m. My head started feeling light and I was feeling nauseated. I was wondering if I was going to get a headache. My symptoms became worse as time passed. At the end of my workday, the feelings were so extreme that I decided it would be best to go home and sleep off my headache.

My daughter Faith which is 10 years old, walked me to our vehicle. She unlocked our van. My head and neck were aching so severely that I thought my head would fall off. She placed me in the driver seat and buckled my seat belt. She ran around to the passenger side and got in and buckled her seat belt. She asked me where the keys were located and I told her in my right pocket. She reached for the keys and found them then started the car. I remember placing the car in reverse and wondering if I was going to run the car through the building behind us. I vaguely remember driving Faith and myself home. Thank God our home is one mile from my work.

On arriving home, Faith had to help me out of the car. I started toward the door and my body was crying to lie down with each step I took. With each step, I thought it would be my last.

When I arrived in my bedroom, my head was throbbing. I fell on the bed and crawled up in the fetal position. I lay in that position for what felt like hours. My pains were connected to my heartbeat because every time it beat, my head would throb. My body was feeling like it didn't belong to me. My neck would not move when I tried to look around.

Fear set into my mind and body. I knew the doctor had told me at my last visit that I had migraines. This was nothing similar to a migraine that I had had previously. My heart was racing so fast I could hardly breathe. My eyes would barely open to see. I thought about it and knew if I died I would go to heaven. I had been saved at the age of nine. I had been asking God to help me. My body would not obey my commands of getting up and moving. Fright and confusion were getting the best of me.

Faith came into my room and asked, "Are you feeling better?" I told her I loved her and I was getting ready to die. She started crying and said, "Mommy, what should I do?" My body wouldn't let me answer her because I was in such pain. While her tears were running down her face, she lay beside me. She held me and told me she loved me. She said, "Please don't die." I felt her warm teardrops on my face.

My son Brock had just arrived home from college. He heard noises upstairs and he was confused because I never was home before him. When he walked quickly into my room, he couldn't believe his eyes. His mouth fell open. I was in a ball position and Faith was beside me crying, "Don't die. I love you."

Faith saw Brock and started to cry more. She said, "I don't know what is wrong with Mom." Brock looked at both of us. His expression on his face could tell all. He was scared and didn't know what to do. Faith turned toward him and said, "I am calling 911." Faith called 911 and answered all the questions that were asked. They would be sending an ambulance, and it would arrive in ten minutes. Faith told Brock that she hoped that the ambulance arrived soon. Faith knew an adult should be with them, and she called her Mamaw Viola to come to our house and stay with them until the ambulance arrived. Viola is my mother.

Brock and Faith were so scared that they were shaking.

It seemed forever until Mamaw Viola arrived. She came in the house swiftly, calling everyone's name. She heard Brock say, "We are upstairs."

Brock and Faith helped me down the stairs. When my children took me downstairs, my legs were like rubber and my body would not function properly. They had to almost carry me. It took all of Brock's and Faith's strength to put me on the couch downstairs. Mamaw Viola placed a blanket over me because my body was shaking so fiercely that my teeth were chattering. Faith told Brock she was going outside to wait for the ambulance.

When Faith saw the ambulance, she was so excited. She ran back inside to tell Brock and Mamaw Viola. She left the garage door open so the ambulance workers could come in. There was a "Hello" and Mamaw Viola said, "We are here, come in." Viola could not believe this was happening to her daughter and family. She looked down at me and I was crying. I said, "I am going to die, let me die."

The ambulance workers asked their questions and everyone tried to answer as best as each one could. All of them were thinking, *Hurry up! Our mom Cheryl never complains about her health!* They knew this was very serious.

The ambulance workers placed me on the stretcher. They started talking to me. I started saying, "Oh, my neck. I can't move my neck. Please don't hit bumps. It hurts worse when you are moving me!" They placed me in the back of the ambulance and closed the doors. Mamaw Viola asked if she could ride in the front and the ambulance worker said, "Yes." Brock and Faith were behind the ambulance, holding on to each other and crying as I was rushed to the hospital. Little did they know that I was very ill and was dying.

Chapter 3

Emergency Room

I could not believe this was happening. I had not ridden in an ambulance since I was four when my mom and I had a car wreck. Now I was forty-eight. It kept running through my mind, *What could be wrong with me?* I had already told the ambulance workers that my neck was one hundred out of ten on a pain scale when they asked how I was. It seemed like the driver hit every bump on the road. I hoped and prayed that they would be at the hospital soon because my mind was making me go conscious and unconscious. It seemed like a dream. I kept praying, "God, please help me." I knew he was with me. On the way to the hospital, Mamaw Viola had called my neurologist, Dr. Aidan, and told him that I would be entering the emergency room around 5:30 tonight. The doctor could prepare the emergency room for me.

We finally arrived at the hospital after thirty-five minutes of extreme pain and suffering because of the movements. The ambulance workers placed me in the emergency room and told the admitting office it sounded like a migraine. I told them, "I don't think so," and they looked at me strangely. I was then placed in an area so the nurses and hospital doctors could examine me. They started asking fifty questions and I said, "Just please make my head and neck stop hurting." The nurse asked the same questions as an ambulance workers had asked. I thought the questions would never stop. Finally the nurse gave me a shot of morphine. I wasn't used to medicine except my migraine medicine. I started feeling as if I were floating and started seeing things in the room. I saw animals and people that were not there. I was hallucinating. I then went into a deep sleep.

The nurse and doctor decided after five hours in the emergency room that I was having a severe migraine attack. When they asked me from one to ten how my head and neck pain were, I answered, "Eight to nine and I can't move my neck." The nurses ignored my response and told Mamaw Viola, "We are not going to admit her to the hospital because she only has a migraine and she needs to sleep it off." I heard the nurses' response and said, "Noises and light don't bother me, but moving my head or neck almost kills me. I don't think it's a migraine." The nurse insisted that it still was a migraine. My mom couldn't believe they were sending me home. The nurse filled out my discharge papers and I was released from the emergency room. It took three people to help me get off the stretcher and placed in the car.

Chapter 4
Going Home

I couldn't believe I was in the backseat of a car going home without answers of why I felt this way. I slept and prayed most of the way home. When we arrived home, my children came out to the car to help me back to bed. My body and mind wouldn't work together. My sons Kent, Brock and Grant literally had to carry me upstairs.

Faith covered me with her favorite blanket that I had gotten her for her birthday. I lay there all night with Faith beside me. I couldn't sleep. Every time I tried to move my neck, it had a sharp pain that went through it and then went through my head. I knew that if this was a migraine, eventually the medicine would start working. However, nothing helped my neck and head this time. After six hours of trying to sleep and asking questions to myself, this was disbelief to my mind. I tried to get up in the morning, but Faith said, "What are you doing?" I said, "I am going to take a shower. Maybe the warm water will make me feel better." Faith agreed and she helped me to the shower. I stood in the shower and let the warm water run on my achy body.

After a few minutes, I tried to bend down to wash myself, but my neck would not move. I thought that maybe I had pulled a muscle in my neck previously. The warm water didn't help me feel better. I got out of the shower slowly and put my clothes on. I was going to work today. I thought that going to work might help me to feel better. Faith asked, "Where are you going?" I said, "I think if I get my mind off my pains, I will feel better." Faith said, "No, I don't agree." I said, "I have to go to work today." I went downstairs and called my mom to come and take me to work. I didn't feel like I could drive. When Mom arrived, she asked if I felt better and I said, "A little." While we were in the car moving, I wondered if I had made the right choice.

I arrived at work at 7:15 a.m. I first saw the room go round and round. Then I started getting chills. I thought maybe I had the flu or a stomach virus. My head and neck were still in tremendous pain. I tried to do my job, but my head felt like some foreign object and it felt very heavy on my shoulders. Next, my limbs felt like Jell-O. When I started falling to the ground, my first thought was to try to hold on to something so I wouldn't fall. However, I fell on a small table. I hit my leg and I was on the ground. Everyone came running to me. I looked up and saw all of their faces. Their expressions were of fright. I guess they were wondering if I was dead. My body was just like a rag doll. I felt cold and numb on the floor.

Several friends lifted me up and helped me walk to my friend Pat's car. My head felt like it weighed a ton. I could not move my head and neck. I was terrified. Did a migraine last this long? Did it make you start thinking rational thoughts? I had never experienced any of these feelings and thoughts until yesterday. Pat drove slowly because I told her, "I am nauseated."

It took five minutes to get home, but it felt like an hour. Pat helped me slowly toward the door. I said, "Take me to the grass because I am going to throw up." We barely made it to the grass. I felt somewhat better after this. This was the time I wished my bedroom was downstairs. The stairs were so difficult to climb. After the stairs, I walked very slowly to my bed. My head and neck were hurting so badly that I told Pat if she would give me pills to knock me out, I would take them, even though in the past medicine was something I rarely used.

I slowly looked at the clock. It was 8:00 a.m. and I was finally home. All of this had happened in forty-five minutes at my job. It seemed like a whole day. I got in bed and Pat covered me up with three blankets, but I was still cold. She found a pan for me to throw up in if I needed it. I told her to leave it near me because I was nauseated again. Pat asked me if I needed her to stay and I told her, "No." But inside me I was crying, "Yes, because I think I am dying."

She placed my phone beside me and told me to call her if I needed anything. I said, "Thanks for everything." I tried to smile but couldn't. Pat left and went back to work.

I had been scared before, but I was terrified this time. I knew that I had to be strong no matter what. I couldn't sleep because of the pain. I needed to go to the bathroom, but it hurt so badly to move that I decided to lie there and not even move my eyes. When I was very still, I felt better. I started to pray. I felt some relief and fell asleep for thirty minutes. I woke up and the clock had passed one hour since Pat left. Time was going very slowly. I had heard that when a person is in pain, time stands still. Now I knew that was true.

I started remembering when my four children were born. Many thoughts went through my head. I thought about the fun things we did together. I had resigned from my job to stay home and raise my children. I will never regret that decision. God had given them to me, so I wanted to be with them. I then started thinking about my mom and dad and how wonderful they were. God had given me great parents.

I wondered if this is what people do before they die. I wondered if you think about all your loved ones, and then I started shaking. I felt like I was going to freeze to death. The room was warm, but I couldn't stop shaking and my teeth couldn't stop chattering. Next, my stomach started to feel very nauseated. *Yes,* I thought, *I'm going to throw up.* I almost did not make it to the pan that was beside me. I couldn't even get up to clean the pan. Yuck!

This went on for seven hours until my mom, Viola, and daughter Faith arrived home. Mom said, "You need to call your doctor." "Why?" I said. "They said it was a migraine. I feel like I have the flu or a stomach virus because I have thrown up six times today. I am also freezing." My mom came closer and handed me the phone and said, "Call the doctor now!"

It even hurt to hold the phone! I dialed the doctor's number and left a message on his machine. I thought, *When he calls back, I will either be dead or passed out.*

Thirty-five minutes later, he returned my call. He started out asking questions and I answered each one. I wanted to scream in the phone, "I can't take much more." I finally told him all about last night in the emergency room. I also told him everything that had happened today. He then said, "Cheryl, you need to come back to the hospital." I frankly said, "No, send me something for pain. I don't want to go back to the emergency room." I had a high tolerance of pain. I had all four of my children naturally, but this was nothing like I had ever experienced. He then said, "This is very serious. I feel this is life threatening." I repeated what he said: "Life threatening?" He answered, "Yes."

I felt like my body had known this since yesterday. I was dying, but I really didn't want to accept it. I asked the doctor if he would call the emergency room and tell them I was coming back. I did not want to wait for hours before they examined me. Dr. Adan said, "I will and I'll come to the emergency room also!" I felt relieved, but I was still scared.

I hung up the phone and told God, "I'm in your hands and I trust you. Please give me the strength to make it back to the emergency room—yes, the same one I went to last night."

My mom, Faith, and Brock all came to my room and asked, "What did the doctor say?" I started crying and said, "I have to go back to the hospital." My son Brock said, "I will take you in my car! No need to call an ambulance this time!" I looked at him and saw the love in his eyes. I reached for him and he hugged me and said, "Mom, I love you." Faith was beside me and touched me and said, "Everything will be all right."

My mom was holding my back while Brock and Faith were on each side of me. They talked to me as we walked down the dreaded stairs. Once down, I couldn't even look around because of the severe pain in my head and neck. I could only look forward. A thought came in my mind: *Don't look back. Always look forward, and everything will be okay.*

That was a message from God.

Chapter 5

Emergency Room Again

B rock placed me very gently in the back of his car. Faith rode in the back with me and my mom rode in the front with Brock. Brock tried to miss the bumps on the road, but when he hit one I would say, "Ohhh!" Brock drove fast with his blinkers on. We finally got to the same emergency room that I had been in last night. It had actually been less than twenty-four hours. *Oh well,* I thought. *Dr. Aidan will see what is wrong with me this time.*

I vaguely remember going to the emergency room. I remember being placed on the stretcher and everyone looking at me. I was freezing and shaking. I heard my teeth chattering. My jaws became very sore because of this. The nurse came in and took my temperature and said very loudly, "It's 105 and a half degrees." The nurse looked at me with a surprised look on her face and gave me a shot admittedly. The nurses started talking and asking me the same questions I had been asked last night. I remember saying, "My pain was worse today than last night." I then heard a voice say, "Let's give her something for her pain!" *Yes!* I thought. Then I went into a light sleep.

When I woke up, I had my feet and arms tied to the bed. I was wondering, *Why?* When I tried to turn my head, it would not turn to the left or right. My head and neck were still in severe pain. I heard a familiar voice. My eyes tried to find the voice since my body couldn't move. My eyes found Dr. Aidan's face near me. He looked at me with tears in his eyes. I thought, *Why is he crying? I'm here at the hospital. You can now help me get over the migraine, flu, or stomach virus.*

Dr. Aidan's voice was quiet but firm. He said, "Cheryl, everyone in the emergency room is so sorry." I thought, *Sorry? What does he mean by saying sorry? Oh no, I must be going to die!* "No, please I want out of here!" I said. "I want to see my children and parents. It is not my time to go!" Dr. Aidan continued even though all of these thoughts were going through my mind. I thought, *It's not a migraine?* I heard someone say, "I don't believe this is a migraine." I thought, *Yes, someone is now listening to me.* Last night I told the ambulance workers and nurses I didn't think it was a migraine, and they didn't agree with me.

Dr. Aidan said, "If you hadn't come to the emergency room when you did, you would have died! You had around two hours to live." Then his head went down as he looked at the floor. *What?* I thought. *Two hours? How can that be?* He looked up and said, "You have spinal bacterial meningitis. We took fluid from your spine with the needle and the fluid was not clear; it is infected."

My next thought, after the *two hours to live,* was *A needle in my back!* Oh my! I saw all the nurses and doctors racing around while putting on masks and smocks to cover themselves. This time they were going to admit me to the hospital. They quarantined me.

Spinal bacterial meningitis—what is that? I thought. I had heard of it, but I knew nothing about the disease. *Nothing,* I thought; however, it almost killed me.

Chapter 6

Waking up and Not Seeing

I slept for days. I don't remember anything that happened at that time. I remember waking up in the hospital room and having a cold washcloth on my face. I opened my eyes and everything was blurry for several days. I was so scared. I got upset. The nurse gave me some medicine that made me sleep.

After several days, I opened my eyes and could see clearly. I tried to move my arms, but they were still tied to the bed. An IV was on the right side of my arm close to my shoulder and I couldn't see where it was going. I called out to my mom, and she came to me. I said, "Where is the IV going?" Then she said, "It is a pick and it is going to your upper part of your arm, running close to your heart." "A what?" I said. My mom said, "They are giving you a large amounts of medicine, and a pick is better than just an IV going through a vein. Your veins also collapsed." My next question was, "When will I get to go home?" Mom said, "The doctor says you have to have fourteen days of antibiotics going through your veins." *Oh, I thought, I hope this is a dream.*

It wasn't.

I stayed in the hospital eighteen days. I was allergic to the first antibiotic, and it caused thrush mouth and hives all over my body. I had to have medicine three times per day rubbed on my body for boils, and also I had to rinse out my mouth three times a day for the thrush. They changed my antibiotics, and then I started feeling better.

It was a long eighteen days, but I made a lot of friends and I talked about God to everyone. God had given me the strength to live, and I felt very lucky.

The doctors and nurses came into my room every one to two hours each day. After I awoke, I noticed that I could move my neck and it didn't hurt as much. A physical therapist would help me walk and talk better each day. She was amazed how well I was progressing. I told her, "I have God on my side."

When I got up, I noticed that on my pillow I could see a large amount of my hair. I thought, *I'm losing my hair!* I ended up losing half of my hair, and when I got out of the hospital I had fourteen inches cut off. I hadn't had short hair in eighteen years. I felt so naked on my neck and back without my hair, but that was okay as long as I was alive.

Faith and I were talking one day in the hospital when we looked at each other and Faith said, "It was God's will for you to go to work that day you fell on the floor." I started thinking about it and said, "You are correct. If I hadn't, I would have lain in bed until the headache was supposed go away. However, it would not have gone away. I would have just died. My getting up, falling at work, and not being able to think correctly proved to me it was something else, not a migraine." My mom said, "If I hadn't heard about what had happened at your work, I probably would have let you stay home for a couple of days to sleep off the migraine. I would not have insisted on you calling your doctor." We all three felt God's hands were in this situation. It worked out for the best.

The day before I was released, the doctor came in my room to examine me. I asked, "Is there a shot or medicine I could take when I get out of the hospital that would prevent me from getting spinal bacterial meningitis again?" He told me, "No. There's a 99.9 percent you will not get it again." I just looked at him, and something in my gut did not believe him. I asked him again, and he looked very irritated at me and said, "You will not get this disease again." However, I still felt inside this was not true. He was trying to reassure me that I was wrong. I did tell him my neck was still sore and my head felt as big as a pumpkin. He said, "As time passes, you will feel like new." I thought, *New? I have not felt like new in two years. I hope he is correct.* He seemed to be so sure of what he was saying. He left my room with a smile on his face.

I couldn't sleep the last night I was in the hospital. I was so excited about going home. I thought about home and the saying "There is no place like home." That was very true. You learn to appreciate things more when you haven't had them for a while. The next morning, when the nurse came in my room to remove the pick from my right arm, I told her, "I see the end of the rainbow by going home, praise the Lord." She smiled and told me, "You had a rough road, but you overcame it with God." I smiled and said, "True, very true!"

I had packed the night before. It was time to go home!

Chapter 7

Eighteen Days in the Hospital then Going Home

My mom, dad (Doyle), and Faith came to the hospital to take me home. When they rolled me outside in a wheelchair, the first thing I felt was the sun. Its warmth was soaking in my body. I looked up and saw the blue sky and beautiful, fluffy clouds. The birds were singing. It was wonderful to hear their music. It sounded like they were singing the words "going home, going home." I smiled. The warm air was blowing in my hair. I stood up, and it felt wonderful to be outside. I had been inside for eighteen days, and I had missed the summer's warm days and nights.

The ride home was very enjoyable. I took in every sight there was. I thought, *Everything I am seeing is God's work.* When we arrived home, my boys met me at the car and held me so tightly. I didn't know if they were ever going to let me go. It was a wonderful feeling, and it was great being home. The doctor said I had to stay away from public places so I would not come in contact with germs for more than four weeks, and this wasn't easy. Everyone had to do all my errands. My sons and my dad always took me to my doctor appointments, and I couldn't drive for four weeks.

I went back to work after six weeks. It was great seeing all my friends. When I went back to my doctor for a checkup, I told him my neck was still hurting. He kept saying, "With spinal bacterial meningitis, it may take six months before your head and neck feel like they did." I listened to what the doctor said, but I really didn't hear him. All I could think about was six months with all of this pain. "Oh, God, please give me strength," I said, and he did.

Chapter 8

Why Is My Neck Hurting?

For thirteen months, I worked and tried to do everything like before, but my neck would hurt every day. I went to the doctor and he said my neck was swollen. He put me on steroids because, he said, steroids would help my swelling. I asked him why I was swollen, and he said, "It is part of getting rid of spinal bacterial meningitis." I looked at him and said, "I think something is wrong." He tried to reassure me nothing was wrong. I still had a feeling in my gut that he was incorrect.

I bought every neck pillow available through TV advertisements to help with neck pain. None of them worked. I then found a person named Deb to massage my neck. I went to her every two weeks. She made my neck feel like it was out of this world. However, after a couple of days my neck would start causing me pain again. Deb recommended for me to visit a chiropractor. I had never been to one. I had also heard positive and negative things about this chiropractor. I decided I would give him a chance. I hoped it would relieve my pain.

He worked on my neck and it felt better. Just like the massage, it didn't last over a couple days and then it started hurting again. I thought, *What is wrong with me?* Everyone I went to kept checking my neck but told me it was still healing. Then, they would give me medicine to try to relieve my pain. I was not a person who usually took medicine; however, this time I would take any medicine to feel better. I prayed for God's will with my neck.

Chapter 9

Sledding in the Snow

Time had passed, and it was January 2011. It had snowed enough for us to get out of school and go sledding. We would ride on our hills behind our house. My children and I always go sledding, even if there is a small amount of snow on the ground. Everyone gets so excited. However, I got up and had no energy.

I made myself prepare breakfast for everyone and then helped my children get on their clothes to go sledding. They saw that I hadn't put on my sledding clothes and asked, "Why don't you have you sledding clothes on?" I told them, "I'm going to stay inside, have hot chocolate with marshmallows ready, and snow cream for you all when you come in." All of my children looked surprised. I had never stayed inside when they were outside sledding. It was fun being outside in the snow with my children.

I knew then something was wrong with me. I called the doctor that day and made an appointment for a checkup. I went several days later to the doctor. He couldn't find anything wrong with me. He did blood work, a CT scan, a CAT scan, a bone-density test, and an X-ray, but he still found nothing. I had a mammogram, but it was also negative. Praise the Lord! However, why was I tired almost all the time, and why was my neck still sore? No one could give me an answer. No one!

Chapter 10

The Beach

Vacation time is such a fantastic time with my family. Kent, Brock, Grant, Faith, my mom Viola, and I were off to Myrtle Beach! When we go on vacation, I am the one that usually drives. It is so relaxing to get in a car, pray, and sing on our way to our destination. This time it was different. My neck would start hurting, and then we would have to stop more times than normal so I could get out of the car, walk, and massage my neck. I moved my neck to the left and right, and then sharp pains would run down it.

When we arrived at the beach, I just wanted to sit down and look at the ocean. I usually wanted to walk, but not this time. The drive had taken all of the energy I had. On this vacation, I walked in the morning and relaxed the rest of the day. This was not me. I kept asking myself, "Am I ever going to be an energetic person again?" I prayed I would. My whole family kept asking me to go and do this or go and do that. I kept saying, "No, I just want to rest." My mom,

Viola, knew something was wrong. I always played in the sand, and I always did what the kids wanted to do; but not on this vacation.

My mom said, "As soon as we get back home, you are going to the doctor." I said, "For what? They said there is nothing wrong with me and I'm getting over the spinal bacterial meningitis that I had last year." We both sighed and dropped the subject. But I knew I had to make an appointment later and talk to the doctor about this again.

Chapter 11

Doctor's Opinion, Not Mine

Each morning when the alarm went off, I thought, *Oh, no, I can't get up.* But I said a prayer, went off to my daily routines, and then went to work. I worked each day in pain, went home, and put either heat or ice on my neck. In several days, I had another appointment with my doctor for a checkup. I went into the doctor's office thinking he would just give me more medicine for my pain. Everyone thinks medicine will cure all aches and pains. The doctor examined my neck and said it looked better. I, however, looked at him and said, "But it doesn't feel better." He said, "Give it time." Time, time, time—that is all the doctors could say.

I left the doctor's office with a lot of unanswered questions. Time went by, I still had headaches, and my Neck still hurts.

I eventually made another appointment in October for a checkup. I was going to the doctor every two months after my first case of spinal bacterial meningitis. The doctor asked if I was still having headaches, and I replied, "Yes, mostly small ones, but once a week I have a severe one." I kept telling him, "I can look at light, and sounds don't bother me. When you can't, those are symptoms of a migraine."

Then I told him, "I don't think it is a migraine. I have to keep something in my stomach all the time. Food and liquid help my headaches subside for around thirty minutes." He looked at me very strangely and said, "I've never heard of that. Keep taking your migraine medicine if it helps your headaches ease off." I told him, "Sometimes it does and sometimes it just eases the pain." He asked about my neck, and I said, "It still hurts." He examined me by making me move my neck in different directions. I could do what he asked, but I kept telling him it was sore. He said, "It looks like the swelling has gone down since last month." I looked at him and asked, "How long will my neck be in pain?" He said, "It should go away soon." I thought, *Soon? When is soon?*

Chapter 12

Saturday Morning That Changed My Life

Friday was a normal day at work—busy but enjoyable. At the end of my workday, Faith came by my classroom and asked, "When are we going home?" I said, "Now." When we arrived home around eight, it was movie and popcorn night. Faith selected the movie while I popped our popcorn. The aroma of the popcorn didn't smell tasty like it usually did. This was strange to me.

We sat down and started watching the movie. I fell asleep during the movie. Afterwards, Faith woke me up. We walked upstairs and went to bed. We said our prayer and read the Bible like we do every night. I remember waking up in the middle of the night with a small headache. I got up and went to use the bathroom. After this, I went slowly back to bed. My head pains were getting worse.

Earlier, I had set my alarm clock for 6:30 a.m. because my youngest son, Grant was going to take an ACT test at his high school. I always prepared all of my sons a good breakfast before any tests they took. When the alarm went off, I couldn't get up because my head and neck were severely hurting. I waited five minutes before I got up, then I made myself get out of bed and go open the bathroom door. Once I was in the bathroom, I opened the drawer and got my migraine shot that I took for headaches. I opened the package and placed the shot on my leg. It stung, but I would take anything to stop the pain of a headache.

I was hoping this whole time that I would get better so I could prepare Grant's breakfast. I sat down for five more minutes hoping the shot would go into effect soon. I heard Grant in the other bathroom. I got up and felt very dizzy and nauseated. I walked slowly toward the door and saw Grant near the bathroom. I said, "Grant," and he turned around and looked at me. He said, "Mom, what is wrong with you? Your eyes look like a wild animal's or a scared person's. You are so pale, Mom." I told him, "I am fine," because I didn't want him to get upset before his test.

I really needed to go back to bed. I prayed with Grant about his ACT test. I told him, "You will do great! Just do your best, and I will see you at home after the ACT test. I will have lunch ready when you come home." Then I hugged him and told him, "I love you and I am praying for you." That is the last thing I remember from Saturday morning—until Tuesday evening. My head was in such severe pain that my body blocked the pain from my mind. I never prepared lunch for Grant.

Chapter 13
No Memory

Faith and my mom are my memory from Saturday morning until Tuesday evening. When I woke, I kept asking the doctor, "Why can't I remember?" and he said, "Your body had you to block out the pain of the past four days." Faith said after Grant left that I came back upstairs to check on her. Then I said, "I am going outside to walk." I changed clothes and got Gracie, our golden retriever. She walked with me every day. I usually walked around thirty-five To forty minutes a day. However, this Saturday my head and neck hurt worse every step I took.

I came in early and told Faith I didn't feel like finishing my walk. I went and took a shower. After the shower, I felt like if I lay down then my head would feel better. This did not happen. Faith decided to lie down beside me. Each time she moved, she said I would tell her, "Don't move the bed because it hurts my head." Faith said, "I'm going to call Mamaw Viola. I said, "No! I will feel better after I lay here a while." Even though I told her not to call my mom, Faith did. Faith told her that I had a migraine and Mamaw Viola told her that she would be here in five minutes. I'm glad Faith didn't obey me this time.

Faith helped me up from the bed and helped me put my clothes on. She then helped me down the steps. Faith said in her mind she knew I had spinal bacterial meningitis again. She put me on the couch, and I curled up in a ball. I was crying, "I want to die. It hurts so bad I want to die." Brock was asleep upstairs and heard me yelling, "I want to die!" He got up and ran downstairs. He found me on the couch. He got a blanket and placed it over me because I was chilly. He looked at Faith and said, "Is this really happening again?" Faith looked at him and said, "I think it is spinal bacterial meningitis again." Brock said, "She just had this last year and we almost lost her then! How can this be happening again?"

Mamaw Viola came through the door and just stared at the situation in front of her. Faith turned to Mamaw Viola and said, "I think it is spinal bacterial meningitis again." Mamaw Viola said, "I hope not. Let's hope it is a migraine!" Even though she remembered me calling her that morning while I walked and told her my head was hurting so badly, I could hardly walk and talk. I had said, "Mom, I am not having a migraine. Light and sound don't bother me. Also, as long as I keep something in my stomach my head feels better." Mamaw Viola asked me, "Have you told the doctor this?" and I said, "Yes, I have told every doctor I have gone to, plus everyone that has looked at my swollen neck!" Mom said, "All right. Walk and call me when you get finished." I never called her. Faith did.

Chapter 14

This Time Will It Be Death?

In the meantime, Faith had called 911 and the ambulance arrived. I was still on the couch telling everyone, "I am in so much pain. I want to die." When I saw the ambulance workers with the stretcher, I told them, "Please give me something to make all of this stop. Please. I think I am dying." The ambulance workers placed me on the stretcher and rolled me into the ambulance. Mamaw Viola knew this time she could ride in the front. She had ridden in the front last year when I had had spinal bacterial meningitis the first time.

The ambulance workers tried to find my veins and they couldn't. I have severe rolly veins. Everyone has trouble finding my veins. Several nurses have blown my veins from previous experiences. While riding to the hospital in the ambulance, my mom called Dr. Aidan's office. Another doctor was on call, and his name was Dr. Ross. Later he called her back. He told my mom he was at home and he didn't know anything about me or my case from the previous year. My mom asked him, "Can you get in touch with Dr. Aidan because I feel it is spinal bacterial meningitis again?" Dr. Ross said, "No, she doesn't have spinal bacterial meningitis again. People don't get it twice." My mom then asked if he could get in touch with Dr. Aidan for the second time. He said, "The emergency room doctor can handle her case until one of us comes to the hospital." My mom said, "Okay, thanks." And then she hung up the phone, thinking he was wrong!

I hadn't had anything to eat that morning, so they said I was dehydrated and it was harder to place an IV in an arm when this happened. My mom Viola said that all the way to the hospital I was crying, "Please stop the pain!" When we arrived at the hospital, they rolled me into the emergency room and the ambulance workers said, "We couldn't get an IV in this patient and it sounds like a migraine." Had they not said this last year and were wrong? I knew they were wrong again.

The nurses tried to get the IV in both of my arms and both of my hands, but they could not get it in. The hospital doctor suggested that they should put it in my neck. They started the pick in my jugular vein of my neck. This stayed there three weeks, and it was on the right side of my neck.

The emergency room workers ran every blood test and body scan on me. They said, "Your white blood cells are normal." They found nothing, but my temperature was 104 degrees and I was chilly. After twelve hours in the emergency room, the doctor told my mother they were going to release me. My mom called my dad to come get us. My dad said, "What is wrong with Cheryl?" Mom said, "They found nothing. I feel like it is spinal bacterial meningitis, but they keep telling me it's not."

They had not tested me yet for spinal bacterial meningitis for the second time. The nurse asked me what my pain was from one to ten. I told her it was a ten out of ten. I kept telling her that my neck was hurting and my head was hurting the same as when I first came in the emergency room. My mom looked at the nurse and said, "I wish you would do something. She keeps complaining of pain." They came in and gave my mom a release form and she signed it. I was on the stretcher still in agony with the pain in my neck and head. Mom thought no one had really helped me. She thought, *When I take her home, is she going to die?*

Chapter 15
The Shot

The emergency doctor told the nurse to give me a shot for pain before they sent me home. The nurse went and got the shot and injected me. Mom later said I looked like I went to sleep after the nurse gave me the shot. My mom was worried. She couldn't wake me. She touched me and tried to pull me up. No response. She called for the nurse, and eventually she came into the room. My mom told the nurse, "After you gave her a shot, she went to sleep." All of a sudden, I rose up and pushed my mom and said, "I want to go home." My mom said my eyes had the look of wild animal's and also looked glassy. After I looked at her, I lay back down. No movement after this. No response.

The nurse told the doctor what happened. He said that the shot was too strong for me. The nurse had given me a normal amount for an adult, but it was too strong for me. (Yes, because I slept for five days.) My mom said that I wet myself. She said I kept crying, "Oh, Mama, oh, Mama." My mom Viola said that it broke her heart because she could not do anything to help me. I would also call out, "I want my children. I want to see my children. I want my daughter!" However, I didn't respond to them when they came in and were beside me, talking to me. I didn't even know they were near me.

The emergency doctor finally said, "We had better do more testing. Something doesn't seem right." Mom said, "Please do a spinal bacterial meningitis test." After all of the hours in the emergency room, he finally agreed. My mom went down in the lobby and prayed the whole time. She saw several nurses and doctors going to the room where I was located.

After ten minutes, which seemed like a lifetime to her, the doctors and nurses came to her. The look on their faces told Mamaw Viola everything. She knew before they confirmed the test results to her that it was spinal bacterial meningitis. The doctor opened his mouth to confirm her suspicions. He said, "You are correct! I am so sorry. We should have had her on antibiotics when she first came to the emergency room. We are now, as I speak, putting her on antibiotics for her spinal bacterial meningitis." He then told her mom, "From now on when you bring Cheryl to the hospital and she's complaining about a headache, tell them she's had two cases of spinal bacterial meningitis in less than fourteen months and that they should do that test first. The secret of this disease is to start antibiotics as quickly as you can. Time and antibiotics are the two easy essentials to helping a person live through spinal bacterial meningitis. Spinal bacterial meningitis causes deafness, blindness, and memory loss. Since Cheryl had this disease last year, I can't tell you if she will wake up or even live."

Mamaw Viola was stunned. She wanted go back and see me. She started praying even harder.

She got her cell phone and started calling my children and told them that the doctor said I might not live this time. My children said they were on their way back to the hospital. They had left when the emergency doctor had released me earlier. They thought I was getting better. They were all concerned. They started praying and saying to God, "Please don't take our mother. Please don't." They got in touch with their friends and asked them to start praying for me. They also called different churches that their friends went to and asked them to start praying for me because I was dying. Between my mom and my children, the whole neighborhood and community were praying for me.

The emergency room doctor admitted me. They placed me in NICU at 2:00 a.m. Sunday morning. Sixteen hours passed. They put up signs for quarantine. I stayed in NICU until Tuesday and there were certain visiting hours. Next, they placed me in IMCU until Wednesday. When I was placed in IMCU, my family could spend the night with me. There was a large lounge my family stayed in. My family slept on the recliners in the lounge. Then on Wednesday I was placed in a room.

My mom sang songs to me trying to get me awake. She sang "Jesus Loves Me," "Oh How I Love Jesus," and "Amazing Grace," but still no response. She rubbed my arms, face, and hands. Still no response. My mom, Faith, Kent, Brock, and Grant all got in a circle and started to cry. It was hard for them to see me in this situation. I was just lying there with no response. Then the preacher came in, and all of my children said a prayer with the preacher. They prayed the Lord's Prayer and also a prayer for me.

I had a lot of visitors who came in and prayed for me during this time. There was still no response from me. When everybody talked, touched, or prayed for me, I did not move. I just lay there. There is nothing that I remember from this time. I woke up Tuesday evening and looked around. Nothing was familiar to me. I then saw my mom and asked her, "Where am I?" And she answered, "In the hospital." I thought, *In the hospital? Why was I in the hospital?* Then I fell back into a coma. I was in a no-response state again.

Chapter 16

The Awakening

On Wednesday, I was placed in a hospital room in the spinal wing. I was still unconscious. My family could visit me at any time and spend the night. I could hear voices. They seem to be far away. I heard my name being called. "Cheryl, Cheryl." I also heard, "Mom, Mom. Mom we are all here." I tried to open my eyes, but I couldn't. My body wouldn't let me. I still was hearing voices. They were talking about me, things I didn't understand. I was in the hospital? I was in a coma? I would or would not wake up? I had spinal bacterial meningitis again? No way! They couldn't be talking about me, because I was fine.

I had spinal bacterial meningitis last year and stayed in the hospital eighteen days. I couldn't have spinal bacterial meningitis again! No, they couldn't be talking about me. I had worked Friday and was going to work this weekend. My neck had been hurting and I was tired, but everything else seemed fine. I tried to move my hands and feet, but they were tied to the bed. *What? Why are they keeping me tied? What is wrong with me? This is a dream and I will wake up in the moment.* I waited. No such luck. Now I remembered. Mom had told me that I had spinal bacterial meningitis again. I wanted to die. *I can't die! I have to live for my family. Who will take care of my family? I have to live!*

I prayed for God to help me. I prayed for strength. I tried to open my eyes. I could hardly see when they finally opened. I could only open them a small amount. Praise the Lord, they were finally opening! When they did, I tried to look at my hands. They were still tied to the bed. *Oh my! Those are my hands?* I thought. *Has my mind gone into someone else's body?* My hands and legs didn't look like mine. They were swollen. I tried to lift my legs, and they were still tied down. All I could see were big legs in socks. I could hardly move my body. It was like my mind was not controlling my body, but why? Why was I here?

I was still hoping to wake up from this terrible dream. I thought that if I talked then I would. I tried to talk, but it was a whisper. I tried harder to talk, and I finally got out, "I am awake." My mom and my children came running to me. I heard my mom say, "We need to tell the nurse and the doctor she is awake. My daughter is awake!" I knew that this was not a dream. It was real! Everyone started talking and asking me questions. My family started hugging me and kissing my forehead. I finally asked, "Help me remember why I'm here." Mom came to me and said, "You don't remember?" I said, "No, I just remember I wanted to die, but I don't anymore!"

Mom leaned over me and said, "You have spinal bacterial meningitis again." I said, "How in the world did I get this again? Why do you have me tied down to my bed like a prisoner?" Mom explained to me that the nurses had tried to start an IV and they couldn't find a vein except in my neck. She also said I kept telling the nurses I was going home and going to work. I kept telling them I couldn't miss work! That is why they tied me to the bed. I was trying to leave and pull out the IV.

The nurse came in, and the first thing I asked her was, "Please, can you untie my legs and arms?" She made me promise I would not try to get up or take the IV out of my neck. "I promise, I promise," I said. She removed the ties from my legs and arms, and I said, "Praise the Lord." After she removed them, I could not move my legs but I could move my arms. I got scared. I told the nurse my legs would not move, and she said, "That is normal. A Patricia Neal worker will come work with you in a couple of days." I thought, *Patricia Neal? That is a rehabilitating place. Why will they come work with me? Is my body that bad? Oh, this can't be happening to me.*

I lifted my arms and hands. They were covered with holes and bruises. They were swollen, and I could hardly see my skin for all the black, blue, and green bruises. I said, "Mom, my arms and hands look awful." She agreed but said, "They will get better." I knew she was correct, but I had only been awake for less than thirty minutes, and all of this information was hard to put into my mind at one time. Also, my elbows were sore. I pulled up my arms and looked at my elbows. *What?* I had large sores on my elbows. I asked Mom, "What happened here?" Mom said, "That is when you were trying to get out of the bed. Your elbows were rubbing against the bed sheets."

This was unreal to me. I must have been in a wild state of mind. My mom looked at me and said, "You kept telling everyone that you were going to work, you were going home, and you needed to leave. When you have your mind made up, you know what you do, you do it. That is why they tied you down—so you wouldn't get up and leave." We both looked each other and laughed. Mom started crying and held my hand and said, "That is the first time I have heard you laugh in a long time." We both smiled at each other.

I told mom everything was going to be okay because God was with us. All of this information was hard for me to process clearly. What would be the next information I would learn?

Chapter 17

Will My Body Work?

Several hours later, I woke to a nurse taking some blood from me and checking my temperature, heartbeat, and blood pressure. The hospital workers were great, although I never could sleep. But that was okay because they were very caring and loving. I looked around the room. My children had left, but my mom was still there. I asked her if she had notified my job where I was, and she told me she had taken care of all the calls and all the paperwork for my job.

She is a jewel to me.

God was good to me. He gave me a wonderful mother. I asked Mom, "How long do I have to stay here this time?" She said, "I don't know." Just then, Dr. Terry, the disease doctor, came in and stated that she couldn't believe I was here again. Then she started asking me questions. My head was still feeling fuzzy, and I still had a headache. I asked for something to make my head stop hurting. Dr. Terry said, "We can give you morphine." I asked for something less powerful.

She told me, "Drink black coffee with caffeine in it and that should help you." I asked, "Why coffee?" and she said, "The caffeine helps your muscles relax; this will help a headache." I hated coffee. I didn't like the taste. However, I started drinking coffee and drank it until I left the hospital. It did help my headache some. Not all the way, but it did give me some relief.

I told the doctor, "We have to find out this time how I'm getting spinal bacterial meningitis," and she agreed. I told her, "I am not leaving this hospital this time until we find the problem. Last year I asked for medicine or a shot so I would not get spinal bacterial meningitis again, and every doctor told me I would not get the disease again. Even though I kept telling the doctors before I left that I felt like my head was still fuzzy and my neck was still hurting." Dr. Terry just looked at me. I told her my ear felt different, and she said she would send a doctor to look at my ear. She said, "He will know more about the ear than I would." I told her "Thanks," and she left.

I said a prayer and felt better. The nurse came in and said, "I need to empty your bag." I said, "What bag?" She said, "Your catheter bag." I said, "Oh no, please tell me I don't have a catheter!" She said, "Yes, it has been there the whole time you have been here." I said, "Please take it out!" She informed me she couldn't until I could get up and go to the bathroom with someone helping me. I asked her, "Could we try it now?" and she said, "No." When she left, I moved the covers off my legs and cried. My legs, ankles, and feet were severely swollen.

I tried to move my legs and feet and could not. I thought, *Why am I so swollen?* My arms and hands were swollen when I first woke up. I found out later that my body was shutting down and that is why my body became swollen. It wasn't working correctly. Now they were decreasing in size because I had been exercising. I started feeling my skin, which was so dry. I hadn't had a shower in a week. My skin felt like snakeskin. It was so rough. Also, my mouth and teeth felt dirty. I ran my tongue over my teeth, and my gums hurt. I found out later it was because I hadn't brushed my teeth in a week. I had been in the bed in a no-response state. What was so sad was that I didn't care. All I wanted was for my head to stop hurting and for me to go home. I had been hurting the whole time I had been awake.

The first step was to get the catheter out. I thought that if I got the catheter out, I could start exercising my legs. I decided to exercise in bed even though I couldn't get up. For two days, I exercised my legs and feet. It was hard, and sometimes I almost gave up, but God had saved my life for a reason, and I wasn't going to give up on my legs and feet. I was going to fight it no matter what. I would be able to stand when the worker from Patricia Neal came. I wanted to show her that I could stand.

When the Patricia Neal worker came, she asked me to move my arms and hands, and I did. Next, she asked me to move my legs, and I did. She was amazed. She said that the last time she had come in, I couldn't move my legs. I said, "I have been exercising them every day." She just couldn't believe her eyes. She said, "You are doing wonderful." I told her I had said an extra prayer each time I was exercising my legs. She looked at my legs and had me move them in different ways. She said, "You want to walk?" I burst out, "Yes! Please!" She said, "Let me go get the nurse to take your catheter out, and we will walk to the bathroom." I said, "Now?" She smiled and said, "Yes."

She went out the door, and I was so happy. I couldn't wait until the nurse came back. I couldn't wait to walk again. It had seemed forever since I had walked. Actually it had been one week.

Where was the nurse? *Please hurry,* I thought. I was not being patient. In came the nurse, and I was so excited. She removed that awful catheter. The nurse and the Patricia Neal worker helped me sit up. My body was so stiff and sore. I sat on the side of the bed for about five minutes. I was a little dizzy. I asked the nurse, "Why?" and she said, "That is normal because you haven't been up in a week." I still had the pick in my neck, so we would have to roll the IV pole with us. The Patricia Neal worker put a belt around my waist. I asked her, "Am I a puppy with a leash?" She laughed and said, "No, this is how I can hold on to you in case you were to fall. This is to prevent you from falling." At first, my legs would not stand. My legs felt like they didn't belong to me.

The Patricia Neal worker and nurse helped me move one leg at a time toward the bathroom. It was eight steps, but it seemed like a mile. When I reached the bathroom, I was worn out. After this, she let me walk around the room. I did fine, but it was so hard. I thought it would be easier since I was moving my legs, but I was surprised. It took all of my strength to move my legs. A week ago I had been power-walking forty minutes a day, but now I couldn't even walk by myself. This made me a little sad for a moment.

The Patricia Neal worker helped me back in bed. She said, "You did a great job, and I will be back tomorrow for more walking." I thought, *Great. I feel like a child.* She looked at me and knew I was not very happy. She told me that I was very lucky to be alive since I had had spinal bacterial meningitis twice in fourteen months. She said, "I have seen several cases where the patient couldn't walk, see, hear, or had lost memory after they woke up from this disease. Also, I have seen patients die with this disease." I looked at her and said, "Sorry. Thanks for the story." I thought, *I won't have a pity party anymore.* "I thank God I am alive and that I'm doing better each day." She smiled and said, "That is what I want to hear." She gave me a high five and left.

I thought, *I have all my body parts. They might not be working like I want them to; however, I have them. With time and exercising,*

I'll be able to walk and move like I used to before this disease. No more feeling sorry for myself. I praised the Lord because I was alive. I was a very lucky person.

Chapter 18

Fountain in That Ear

That night I called the nurse every two hours so I could go to the bathroom. I was walking better each time. It was wonderful getting up and getting out of bed. I knew tomorrow I was seeing Dr. Ton, the ear specialist. I had been complaining that my right ear was hurting. Last year when I was in the hospital for the first time having spinal bacterial meningitis, I told the doctor my ear was bothering me. I kept complaining about it. The ear doctor looked at it and said, "It's a little swollen, but it looks okay." Later we found out that was the cause of the two cases of spinal bacterial meningitis.

I woke up early Friday morning. I was exhausted, but I was ready to see the doctor. The pain in my head was getting worse, and the pressure in my ear was causing me to become dizzy. I couldn't wait to get relief. After breakfast, the nurse came to my room with a wheelchair. They wheeled me to Dr. Ton's office. My stomach was doing flips. They called my name. The nurse wheeled me into the room where they placed tubes in patients' ears. I stood up and sat on the table. I looked at Dr. Ton and asked him what he was doing to me exactly. He first said, "We will be taking special pictures of your ear inside and out. The pictures will show all around your ear and also pictures of the brain." After he explained that, he said, "I will be placing the tube in your ear. It will decrease the pressure in it, and there should be less pain around your head." I listened and said, "Great, let's get it done."

I lay on the table in the hospital gown, hoping not to show all (ha ha). Dr. Ton ran the test, made pictures of my ear, and then made a hole in the eardrum. When he did, liquid came out of the ear like a water fountain. The whole side of my face and neck became wet. Dr. Ton said, "Man, there is a large amount of fluid behind your eardrum." He used a suction device for over five minutes in my ear, and he still couldn't get it all. He said, "The fluid continues to come. I'll go ahead and place the tube in." He did, and the fluid decreased. He put a cotton ball in my ear, and it felt very wet. When I sat up, I asked him, "Why was the fluid continuing to flow out of my ear?" He said, "Your ear had so much fluid behind the eardrum that I don't know how you were walking correctly. There is still a large amount of fluid in your ear, so keep the cotton ball in it."

I pulled the cotton ball out of my ear a few minutes later, and it was already soaked. I placed another clean cotton ball in my ear, and I could feel it absorbing the fluid. Quickly, Dr. Ton said, "Today is Friday. Come back in one week." I said, "I have to stay in the hospital for fourteen days so antibiotic medicines can flow through my veins. It will help remove the spinal bacterial meningitis."

I got off the table and sat back down in a wheelchair. The nurse pushed me back to my room. I asked if I could walk and she said, "No, you will have to wait for the Patricia Neal worker." "Okay," I said, but it really wasn't easy to wait. I wanted to walk right then because I knew I was getting stronger.

I went back to bed feeling a little lightheaded. I had become worse since the tube was placed in my ear. I called the nurse, and she gave me morphine. I didn't want it, because the medicine made me see and think of things that weren't real. It made be hallucinate. While I was taking the medicine, I saw black birds and bats all in my room. I saw people who were not real coming in and out of my room. I became very anxious. When my mom was in the room, I told her to get a piece of paper because I wanted her to write down everything that needed to be done at home, school, and the hospital room. I also told her to write chores for my children to finish. I talked more and tried to get out of bed often when I was on the medicine. Also, I saw a lady and she came in my hospital room, sat on the chair, and looked at me. I couldn't see her face, because she was bright. I told Mom, "I think she is my guardian angel. She came to watch over me." I still felt she was watching me each day I was in the hospital. I felt a feeling of comfort come over me when I saw her.

The medicine did help my headache some. I was dizzy all day today. When the Patricia Neal worker came in, she asked me how I was doing. I told her about the tube incident. She sat me up slowly. I looked down at the floor and saw several pairs of feet. I started to walk, and I had to stop. She asked me what was wrong, and I told her I was dizzy and I was seeing things that were really not there. I said, "I had tubes before, but the dizziness went away shortly after the procedure was over. This has continued all day." She took me to the bathroom and then said I had to go back to bed. I really wanted to walk, but I was getting nauseated. It seemed like every time I moved, more fluid would come out of my ear. That was strange. This had never happened after any of my tube surgeries. I told the nurse and she said, "You need to tell the doctor when he comes in." I was also changing the cotton balls every fifteen minutes.

At first, I was throwing the cotton balls away, and then I decided to keep them so I could show the doctor. When I took a cotton ball out, I could squeeze it and fluid would come out. It was a very scary feeling. I thought, *If I am losing this much fluid, how am I staying hydrated?* I drank a large amount of liquid each day when I wasn't in the hospital. Now in the hospital, I didn't drink as much. When different doctors and nurses came in my room, I would show them the cotton balls. They would look at them and at me like they couldn't believe it. I guess they thought I was crazy.

Everyone told me the fluid would stop eventually. *Well,* I thought, *I hope it does soon. This is tiresome to remove a cotton ball every fifteen minutes.*

I ran out of cotton balls. I had to call the nurse for more. She would bring me some and then ask me, "What are you doing with the cotton balls?" I told her about my ear, and she looked at me and said, "If you need anything else, let me know," and then she left the room. This went on all weekend.

I became irritable. My mouth became dry, and I couldn't think correctly. I couldn't even walk, and I just didn't feel like myself. I knew something was wrong. I was losing so much fluid that it didn't make sense. Why was this happening? Why was there a fountain in my ear?

Finally, on Monday, Dr. Terry, my disease specialist, came in and asked me, "What is going on with your ear and head?" I told her, "My head keeps getting worse and keeps hurting more and more severely. It feels like it's going to explode. My mouth is so dry, my skin has gotten dryer, and my ear has never stopped flowing liquid since the tube surgery." I also told her I was using four cotton balls per hour. "I am dizzy, and I can't think correctly." I told her when the fluid came out of my ear that my skin would burn all the way down my cheek. My pillow was totally drenched. I hadn't slept much since Thursday night. My hair was wet and looked like I had just washed it. This was all from the fluid coming from my ear.

I had a hard time thinking. I told her, "I can't complete my sentences when I speak." She looked at my eyes, skin, and in my ear. She put on gloves and took out the cotton ball that was in my ear and placed it in a container. She put the lid on it and said, "I am going to take this to the lab." The results would be back Wednesday. In the meantime, she said, "I am starting you on liquids 24/7 through your IV. She said, "You are dehydrated, and you have to drink one to two cups of liquid every hour." She said to continue caffeine and that it would help my headaches. The caffeine was making me hyper because I didn't drink it when I wasn't sick.

The doctor told me that I would feel better tomorrow because taking in all the liquids today would help my body to start going back to normal. I told her thanks and gave her a high five.

When she left, I couldn't believe this. What was coming out of my ear? Would it ever stop? Could this liquid be why my head and neck had been hurting for the past fourteen months? I lay in the bed with my eyes closed, praying the test would give us the results of all my unanswered questions.

Chapter 19

One Day of Energy

I woke up early and couldn't believe how I felt. The doctor was correct. I had been drinking water and juice every hour. They also continued giving me liquid through my veins 24/ 7. I felt better today than any other day of the week. I knew it would take two days for the test results to come back. I couldn't wait to tell my family that I felt better. My mom, Viola, had gone to get herself something to eat. l never was alone in the day and never was by myself at night. Someone was with me 24 /7.

I have a great family, and I thank God for them every day. They are the ones who helped me every day. The chair in the hospital that they slept in wasn't comfortable, but they stayed with me anyway. After I ate breakfast, I asked the nurse, "Can I take a shower?" I did not want a sponge bath again. I had them every other day, and I didn't feel clean afterward. I wanted warm water to flow on my neck, back, and all of my body. I wanted to wash my hair and have the water run down my body. We never know how many little things we take for granted and how much we will miss them until they are gone. The nurse looked at me and said, "You have the IV in your neck." Then I asked her, "Can I place a bandage on my neck and my mom will help me with the shower?" My mom told her, "I will be willing to do anything to help Cheryl."

I looked at the nurse for permission to take a shower. I told her, "If I have to beg for a shower, I will." She looked at me and said, "I feel sorry for you, so I will let you take a shower." I was so excited. She asked, "When do you want to take a shower?" Without hesitating, I said, "Now." The nurse left to go get the bandage to cover my IV. While she was gone, I told my mom, "Thanks for everything you have done for me." We kissed each other on the cheek. I had a fantastic mom.

The nurse came in and put the bandage on my neck. She said, "If you need me, just pull the emergency rope in the bathroom." My mom and I said, "Thank you so much!" Then she was gone. My mom helped me take a shower and wash my hair. When I stepped into the shower, all I could think about was the warm water running on my body. It was so wonderful, but little did we both know that I wouldn't be able to wash my hair with water again for over two months. Good thing I didn't have oily hair.

After the shower, I put on a clean gown. Also, my mom and I had just put clean sheets on the bed. I was feeling great. I asked my mom, "Can we go for a walk around the inside of the hospital?" She said, "Yes," and I went around twice. I went back to the room. I wanted the room to be neat, so I cleaned up a little. After this, I sat in a chair for the first time since I had been in the hospital.

The nurse came in and said, "I never see you watching TV!" I told her, "I don't watch TV here or at home unless it is something my children are watching. The only thing I have watched at the hospital is the *In Touch* program on Sundays. I watched it every Sunday and learned so much about the Bible. She said, "I like to watch that program too!" We both smiled at each other.

The Patricia Neal worker came in and asked me, "Are you ready to do some exercises?" I said, "Let's go for it!" She smiled. I told her everything I had done today, and she was impressed. I did all my exercise moves and walked with her. She then told me to slow down because I was walking too fast. After that, she said, "Cheryl, I am releasing you from the rehabilitation center. You have improved so much, and I am so proud of you!" I was very excited.

I went back to my room and told my mom what the Patricia Neal worker said. Both of us had smiles on our faces. My mom started kidding me that she would have to put the belt back on me to slow me down. I said, "The dog leash?" We both laughed. I was so happy to be released from the Patricia Neal rehabilitation center. A lot of people had to go there and stay for six months to a year for treatment after they left the hospital with spinal bacterial meningitis. Thank God I didn't have to. God is such an awesome God!

The Patricia Neal worker told me to continue working on my memory and soon I would be back to normal. I gave her a hug and told her, "Thank you for everything!" She left with two thumbs up. "Yes, I'm getting better!" I said to myself. I even called where I worked and told them I would be in next Monday to work. I was so happy that I was feeling better. That whole day was great. I was full of energy. I even walked again that evening. I went to sleep thinking, *Tomorrow I will see the test results. The results will be negative of anything else besides spinal bacterial meningitis and I will get to go home soon.*

I wish that had been true.

Chapter 20

The Test That Changed My Life

I woke up at six o'clock on Wednesday morning to a feeling in my head I had never felt. There was so much pressure that I thought my head was going to explode. I tried to get up, but I couldn't. I called for my mom and told her, "Something is wrong." We called the nurse who then checked all of my vital signs and my blood pressure. My blood pressure was very low. She looked at me and said, "Did you wash your hair today?" I said, "No, why?" She said, "Your hair is totally wet! How?" Then I told her, "My ear must have started draining again."

I looked at my gown, and it was totally drenched. She said, "Dr. Terry will be here soon." I then told her, "Yesterday I felt wonderful, but today I feel the opposite." She helped me up so I could go to the bathroom. I looked at my legs, and they would not work like I wanted them to. *Why? What happened to me in one day to change my body functions?*

After I went to the bathroom, I went back to bed. Dr. Terry came in. She had a look of disbelief on her face. I said, "Good morning," and she said, "Well, I have the test results, and I can't believe it. You have CSF leakage."

CSF leakage? I looked at her puzzled and asked, "What?" She started explaining to me that CSF was the fluid in the brain that was going to the spine and back to the brain. She said, "It isn't supposed to go anywhere else. It is called cerebral spinal fluid. However, you have a leakage, and it is coming out of your ear." Then I asked her, "What are we going to do?" She said, "This morning you are going back to the ear doctor. He is going to take the tube out of your ear, and hopefully this will stop the leakage. This will help you feel better. We have to do more research to find a solution for this problem."

I just looked at her. I couldn't believe this. I asked, "Is this how I got the spinal bacterial meningitis twice?" She said, "Yes! If we don't stop the leakage, you can die." I froze. *Die? I almost died twice already with spinal bacterial meningitis, and now the CSF leakage?*

I had never heard about CSF before. This was a shock to me. My mom went out in the hall with the doctor. She came back into the room and said, "It's time for you to go to the ear doctor again." The nurse was right behind my mom with the wheelchair. It felt like the tube had just been placed in my ear. The ride in the wheelchair to the doctor's office felt like a dream. Cerebral spinal fluid leakage—how in the world did I get this? How would they cure it?

We finally arrived at Dr. Ton's office. My mom signed me in. We went back to the room that had the surgery bed. I got on it and lay down. Dr. Ton came in and said, "I am going to remove the tube, and hopefully this will make the hole smaller." He numbed my ear with some drops. It burned, and my ear felt hot this time. He said, "It is because the fluid is leaking." He looked at my neck and said,

"The leakage has made your neck raw all the way down." When he took the tube out, it started draining more fluid. He said, "I tried to make the hole smaller, but because of the drainage I couldn't. Let's hope with time it will get smaller on its own."

I got up and said, "What is next?" He said, "We have to find someone who will repair your CSF leakage." Then I asked him, "Do you know anyone?" He replied, "No, but I am going to do some research on this." *No one?* I thought. *This is not good at all.* I told him, "Please help me!" He patted my shoulder and said, "I will find a doctor that can help you." I said, "Thanks," and I shook his hand. The nurse and my mom took me back to my room.

My ear was like a fountain. Liquid poured out of it continuously. When I got back to my room, I started drinking water and juice again. I kept thinking of yesterday. How great it was! And then I started thinking of today. There was some sadness. A little amount of time can change anything. I told Mom we needed to pray. She prayed with me, and I felt better.

About an hour went by, and the nurse came in. She told me, "Dr. Terry said you need to be flat on your back and not get up for anything." I asked, "Why?" Then the nurse said, "The doctor said if you are not moving, the fluid will not leak out as much, and this will help you keep the fluid in your body." I asked her, "How am I going to go to the restroom?" and she said, "You will use a bedpan." *Bedpan?* I thought. *Oh my. I had to use it last year when I had spinal bacterial meningitis. I hated using the bedpan because I had to have someone put me on it, and take me off it.*

I'm very independent, but with this disease I can't be. I asked the nurse, "How am I going to eat?" She said, "You'll be on a liquid diet. You will use a straw. You are not allowed to lift up your head. You may turn it slowly left and right, but it has to stay flat." Yesterday I was walking everywhere. Today I couldn't even lift my head. God, please help Dr. Ton to find a doctor that can help me.

I stayed like this day and night. I was so miserable. I would choke whenever I drank liquid even through a straw. My stomach and hernia started burning. They had to give me medicine for that. My hernia hadn't bothered me since the previous year when I had my other case of spinal bacterial meningitis. I wasn't used to sleeping and eating while lying down flat. I always slept on two pillows so my hernia wouldn't bother me. Not anymore.

My mom came over to me and said, "Cheryl, you are strong and you will make it through this." I thought, *I am strong. She's right.* I said to her, "With you and God, I will be able to do this." It was an awful night. Thursday was the same as Wednesday—very rough. I had to be in bed and stay flat. My body wanted so badly to get up and walk. I wanted to go to the bathroom by myself, but I knew I couldn't. When you know you can't do something, you want to do it even more.

The nurse brought my breakfast and said, "After this, I will give you a sponge bath." I told her, "No, thank you." *What? I'm turning down a sponge bath,* I thought. Sometimes they made me feel better, but I told her I didn't feel like it today. I would do it tomorrow. She said, "Okay." Then she left. My mom came to me and said, "Are you okay?" I said, "No. I just want to get well and go home." It had almost been two weeks since I had been in the hospital. I wanted to go outside, feel the sunshine, smell the world, go to work, see my animals, feel better, and be home with my children.

My children came every day to see me, but I just wanted things back to normal. I just wanted to go to sleep in my own bed and walk my dog. I told my mom, "I am acting like a spoiled child, but I'm becoming so sad and I'm asking God, 'Why, why is this happening again?'" I know I wasn't supposed to ask, but I was so sad. I was also in tremendous pain at that moment. The nurse gave me some pain medicine because I was in so much pain with my head that I couldn't think straight. I started crying, "I don't know if I can take this."

I fell asleep with the thought that I am strong. When I woke up, it was almost dark in my room and outside. I called for my mom, but my oldest son, Kent, answered me. He was going to college. He was studying beside me. He turned on the light and said, "Hi, how are you?" I said, "Fine," even though my head would not stop hurting. Also, my back was hurting from lying flat and not moving. The bed was making so much noise that we had to turn it off. It was not very comfortable. I wasn't going to tell him all of my problems. My children had gone through so much just by me getting sick. There were some good things that came from my sickness. We became a closer family, and we learned life is precious and can be taken away in one moment. Cherish what you have and take care of your loved ones every day. Don't take anything for granted. Always put God first. These are things you should do.

I asked Kent, "How was school today? How are you?" Kent laughed and said, "Even though you are in the hospital, you are still concerned about your children and how they are doing in school. That's my mom!" He leaned over and kissed me on the forehead. Then I gave him a big hug. We talked about his day and about life. The nurse came in and gave me my pain medicine. I told Kent goodnight and started to rest. I didn't sleep in the hospital much. I just rested. I thought, *At least I am alive!*

Chapter 21

Who Will Repair My CSF Leak?

Kent went back to studying and then got something to eat. The next morning, before Kent went to class, I prayed with him. After that, he left. I felt the same as the day before: tired and in non-stop pain. No change. After breakfast, Dr. Ton came in and said, "I have found a doctor to repair the CSF leakage. His name is Dr. Wade. He is in Nashville. He wants you to call him before you leave the hospital and make an appointment to see him."

My mom had arrived and said she would call his office today. Dr. Ton said, "Keep doing what you have been doing. I have talked with the hospital doctor, and you can go home Saturday or Sunday." I was excited! However, the disease doctor walked into my room and said, "No!" very loudly. "She will stay here and an ambulance will come and get her; then it will take her to Nashville!" Both doctors looked at each other and walked out of my room. I looked at my mom. "What was that?" I asked my mom.

I heard Dr. Terry, the disease doctor, say, "She will die without the fluid we are giving her. She's losing extreme amounts of fluid each hour. She has to lie flat or the fluid will flow out more." Dr. Ton said, "Okay, it is your call." They said something else, but I didn't hear it. I didn't see Dr. Ton again.

Dr. Terry came back in my room and said, "You are staying here until you go to Nashville." She then looked at my mom and said, "Notify me after you call Dr. Wade's office and find out her surgery date and when she needs to be there. She needs to be there." After that, she told me everything was going to be fine, and then she left. *Fine,* I thought. *I just heard her say earlier that I could die.* I turned, and my mom was already on the phone with Dr. Wade's office. How did she get their phone number so fast?

The office wanted to talk to me. Mom gave me the phone. The office asked me what insurance I had and what my symptoms were. Then his receptionist said, "The earliest Dr. Wade can see you is in a week." "A week!" I exclaimed. "That is too long!" I thought about seven more days like this. I asked her, "Can I see him and then have surgery on the same day?" She said, "Hold one moment, please." I held on to the phone like I was holding on for dear life. She came back on and said, "He can see you on Wednesday next week, and have the surgery on Friday." I said, "Is that the first opening he has?" She said, "Yes."

It was so much longer than what I had hoped for. I thought five days for an appointment and seven days for surgery was too long, but I had to take it. I asked, "If he has any cancellations, can you please call me?" I then gave her my cell phone number and thanked her. I was so disappointed because I had to wait seven more days lying flat on the bed in pain.

I looked at mom and said, "Thanks for calling, but who gave you the number for Dr. Wade's office so fast?" She said, with a smile, "The nurse gave it to me. Everyone here can't believe this has happened to you." I said, "This is a great hospital, and the nurses are fantastic!" I then started to stare at the ceiling, saying, "Surgery, surgery," over and over. I had had so many surgeries on this ear; I wondered if this time would be any different.

Chapter 22

Close to Death

After I finally realized this was real and I was not dreaming, I came to terms with the surgery. I hated being put to sleep and trying to wake up. Next was the getting sick part! I thought of this, and the thought of the CSF leakage came into my mind. I had elected to do the surgery. "Stop complaining," I told myself. "Pray and ask for strength." I had had headaches for almost four years. Some days I didn't even know if I could make it to work. However, praying helped me. Also, I took large amounts of shots and headache medicine.

The day became night. I started becoming nauseated, dizzy, and tired. I told the nurse, and she called Dr. Terry to come check on me. Dr. Terry looked at me and said, "I'll be back tomorrow to check on you." She told the nurse, "Keep fluid going through her, and don't let her get up." I didn't sleep at all that night because of the severe pains in my head and neck. On Saturday morning, I could hardly talk. I couldn't remember things. Dr. Terry arrived and looked at me. She told my mom, "She is getting worse. I am calling Dr. Wade to see if he can see her sooner." When she left, my mom was holding onto my hand. The doctor came back thirty minutes later and said, "Dr. Wade can see you on Monday, and surgery will be on Wednesday. He is out of town and will be back on Monday." *Yes,* I thought. *Two days earlier is better than nothing.*

I motioned "thank you" to her in sign language. She smiled and asked my mom, "Can you come out in the hallway for a moment?" My mom said, "Yes." Then I heard her tell my mom, "She is getting weaker. I don't know if she will make it through the surgery. She has to have the surgery, but be prepared for the worst. The ambulance will be here on Monday to take her to Nashville." My mom then told the doctor, "Brock, my grandson, will drive Faith, my granddaughter, and I behind the ambulance to Nashville."

My mom came back in the room with a sad look on her face. She had tears in her eyes. She told me what the doctor had said about the ambulance, but what she didn't know was that I had overheard the doctor tell her I might not make it through the surgery. I was terrified, but I knew that God was on my side. He had always given me strength.

Saturday night turned into Sunday morning, and I was crying for relief for my head. I drank coffee and took medicine. Sunday was worse than Saturday, and Monday was worse than Sunday. Each day I kept getting worse. I kept getting to where I couldn't think rationally or hold a conversation. My memory was being affected also. Sunday, I lay in bed. I was very still. Every time I had to use the bathroom, I couldn't. I had to use the bedpan. I sometimes wasn't an accurate shooter—ha ha.

I was wishing for Monday to come. It finally did. After Brock and Faith went to school, they came to the hospital. My mom went home and packed some more items for us. We didn't know how long we would be in Nashville. I hated for Brock and Faith to miss school, but they hadn't missed any until I became ill. All four of my children, Mom, Dad, and friends came to the hospital. They wished me good luck, gave me hugs and kisses, and said prayers for me. The nurse gave me pain medicine and a shot for sickness before I left for Nashville. I saw concern and sadness in everyone's eyes. I knew that they thought this might be the last time they would see me alive.

Chapter 23

Ambulance to Nashville

I was waving good-bye to everyone while the ambulance workers rolled me down the hospital hallway. I wanted to cry, but I had to stay strong for my family. I didn't want them to see how scared I was. Inside, I was going crazy with fear. The two ambulance workers were women. They were awesome. They kept fluid going through my veins, and when I got nauseated they gave me a bag.

It was a three-and-a-half-hour ride from one hospital to the other. My mom, Brock, and Faith followed behind the ambulance to Nashville, Tennessee. When I got sick, I would close my eyes, try to pray, and rest. When the ambulance hit a bump, I thought my head would blow off my shoulders. There was so much pressure. Movement made my pains worse.

When we finally got to the hospital, I couldn't believe my eyes. It was enormous! It was bigger than any other hospital in Knoxville. They rolled me straight to my room. The hospital in Knoxville had called, and this one had prepared a room for me before I arrived. It was a very nice room. I couldn't say much about the first hospital doctor who came in my room in Nashville. He came in and asked me, "Why did you come here in an ambulance, and is that water on all the cotton balls?" Before I could explain my situation to him, he said, "I am getting off work soon and another doctor will be in here." Then he was gone. I looked at my mom and said, "What was that? I didn't even get to answer his questions. We must have gotten him at a bad time." Then we all laughed!

The nurse came in and checked me into the hospital. I told Brock; my mom, Viola; and Faith, "Go find a hotel room. Come back here after you check in. I am fine by myself. I am not going anywhere," and I laughed. After they left, the nurse asked me questions that seemed to last forever. After that, I finally slept around thirty minutes. Then another doctor came in and asked me more questions. He told me Dr. Wade would come see me tomorrow. I said "Thanks," and he left. It was finally quiet, but not for long. Another nurse came in and looked at the IV in my neck. She said, "I will take this out tomorrow and place it in your arm." I said, "Why?" She said, "You are not supposed keep that in your neck over a week." I said, "It has been in my neck seventeen days." She replied, "That isn't good," and then she left.

Oh great! Tomorrow I'll be picked and poked at again, I thought. The bruises on my arms and hands were looking better after two weeks. Well, I thought, at least it will be out of my neck. Faith came back in my room and said, "We got a nice hotel close to the hospital. It is five minutes away. Mamaw Viola and Brock are there getting ready for bed." I told her, "Try to get some sleep." We both looked at the chair that she would sleep in. She sat down and said, "It feels better than the other hospital chair." Faith prayed and we both tried to sleep. The nurses were like the other hospital's nurses. They were in your room every two hours to check on you and your vitals. The time seemed to go by so slowly. I couldn't wait to meet Dr. Wade. He was the one that was going to do my surgery and help me become a different person. I thought, *I hope he has the right answers.*

Chapter 24

The Answers

Finally it was morning and I thought, *Yes, answers!* I was still flat on my back. The leakage was worse than ever. Even though I was still flat on my back and not moving, the whole top of my bed was wet. All of my pillows and gowns were soaking wet. My head had extraordinary pain. When the nurse came in, I showed her everything. She was amazed. She asked me, "Are you drinking water?" I told her, "Yes, I am drinking one cup per hour." "The doctor will be here soon," said the nurse.

One hour later, Dr. Wade came in my room with and an enormous smile on his face. He was tall, slim, and in his mid-fifties. He introduced himself and said to me, "Nice to meet you. We couldn't find your DVD and pictures of your test at first, but we have just found them. They were on the nurse's desk. I have looked at your reports, and you have a severe case of CSF leakage." He had done several surgeries to repair CSF leakage. "The surgery I am going to do on you is major. I feel comfortable performing the surgery on you to close up your leakage." I was happy to hear that.

He said to me, "Tell me all about your ear and all the surgeries you have had on it." I looked at him and said, "For twenty-nine years, I have been to six doctors in the United States—north, east, south, and west. They looked at me and told me it was my Eustachian tube. I have had eight surgeries on my ear." He asked, "Have they gone behind your ear or through your ear? I said, "All they have gone through is my eardrum. He jumped up and said, "Well, tomorrow you will be having surgery another way." I looked at him and said, "Please explain your procedure." He said, "I am going to cut behind your ear from the top to the bottom. I will pull the ear back and go through the opened part. I will repair the CSF leakage and anything else that needs repairing. I said, "Well, I have heard my heartbeat for twenty-nine years. If you can fix it, that would be wonderful! Plus I hear my breathing, there is pressure in my ear, and I can hear my intestines make a sound every so often." He looked at me in a very strange way. He said, "Let me look at the pictures again that they took of your ear. I will get back to you."

He came over to me and asked, "Can I take a look in your ear?" I said, "Sure." He looked in it and said, "You have a large amount of fluid coming out of here. Do you have a headache? Are you dizzy or nauseated?" I said, "Yes, all the above!" He went to tell the nurse to put a "cup" on my ear so I wouldn't have to change the cotton balls every ten minutes. I said, "That will be wonderful!" He told me, "I will check the pictures again and be back tonight." When he left, I looked at my mom and said, "He seems to know what he's doing." My mom nodded.

The nurses came in with the *cup*. They secured it around my head with Velcro so it would be secure. The cloth inside the cup absorbed the fluid that was coming out of my ear. This was so much nicer than the cotton balls. I didn't have to change it every ten minutes. I changed it every two hours. I told the nurse, "Thanks!"

I lay back waiting for my children to arrive, but only Dr. Wade came. He was bouncing like a bunny and had a large grin on his face. He said, "I know what has been wrong with you for the past twenty-nine years!" I just looked at him. He continued by saying, "The bone in your ear is not attached correctly, but I can correct that. When I operate on your ear, I will lift up part of your brain to repair the CSF leakage. I will repair the bone problem. If the brain is down too far, I won't be able to do this procedure, but if the brain is in the correct spot, I will be able to fix both problems. I will also remove any scar tissue from the previous surgeries, and I will repair the hole in your eardrum. All headaches will subside."

I looked at him and started to cry. "I have had headaches for almost four years. I have taken medicine for the headaches that has interfered with my liver, stomach, weight, and bones. I have taken prednisone for three and a half years to help the fluid in my ear." Prednisone is a steroid. Steroids interfere with your bones. "I am having trouble with my hip bones because of the steroids." *No headaches? I won't know what to do.* I told him, "You were sent by God to help me. He just smiled. Then he said, "The surgery is tomorrow. Don't eat or drink after midnight." I said, "I haven't eaten solid foods in a week and a half. I have been on my back that whole time too." He said, "After tomorrow, that will change." He started walking out the door and before he could leave my mom said, "Thank you. We are glad we came here." He said, "I am too," and he walked out the door.

I looked up at my mom and said in an excited voice, "I am in shock. Is this true? Oh, it would be wonderful not to hear my heartbeat and hear myself breathe and talk." I then remembered what Dr. Terry had said about me being so weak that she thought I might not make it through the surgery. I didn't feel like I was going to die now. I felt like God was going to give me strength to have the surgery. God helped the doctors in Knoxville to find Dr. Wade, and I knew I would wake up with a repaired ear. Praise the Lord.

My children came in, and I told them what Dr. Wade had told me. They were so excited. Faith said, "Mom, it will be wonderful to see you feel better," and then she hugged and kissed me. "It will," I told her. "It sure will."

The nurse came into my room to change the cup on my ear. Each time a different nurse changed it, she would say, "Oh my! I can't believe this. You are losing a large amount of fluid!" Each nurse would also make sure that I was drinking plenty of liquid. The IV fluid had been going in me for twelve days, 24/7 nonstop.

That night, I couldn't sleep. Tomorrow was the big day! I was so excited and scared at the same time. I thought about going home and not having headaches or a heartbeat in my ear. I had to have noise all the time at work and at home so I could block out the sound in my ear. Not doing that anymore would be wonderful! A quiet room? I wouldn't know what to do. For twenty-nine years I had needed sound wherever I went. I prayed that my brain would be in the correct spot so Dr. Wade could repair anything that was wrong.

The clock wouldn't go fast. Every time I looked at it, the time had only changed fifteen minutes. Eleven o'clock in the morning was when they were supposed to come and get me for surgery. The nurse came in at 2:00 a.m. and said, "Have you had a bowel movement lately?" I said, "No." I thought, *How could you when you are flat on your back for twelve days or when you only had liquids?* She said, "You will have to try." I tried with the bedpan, but nothing happened. Flat on your back trying to do number two? Ha ha. We take a lot for grated when we are well. The nurse then recommended a "toilet chair" beside the bed. I told her I was not supposed to get up. She said, "You can't strain after surgery, so we need you to do this now." She got me up very slowly, and I got so sick and dizzy. I sat down, and she left me so I could have some privacy. *Privacy,* I thought. I hadn't had any privacy or modesty for almost three weeks. Everything had changed with my body since I had been in the hospital. I didn't care about my looks, because when a person almost dies and has headaches as severe as I did, looks are not really that important.

God has made our bodies for us to be happy, not sad with pain. I had to sit on the toilet chair until the nurse came back. Ten minutes later, she finally came back and I said, "All is good." She said, "Great. I will write that on your chart."

She helped me back to bed. I felt like I was going to pass out. She asked, "Are you okay?" and I said, "No, I think I'm going to throw up." I almost threw up, but when I was pregnant I was so sick the whole nine months that I learned how to swallow my vomit. That is what I did this time. It was gross, but at least my head couldn't hurt any worse. When I throw up, it makes my head hurt and my hernia burn. I didn't need that. I felt better when I was flat on my back, even though my back ached because I had lain on it for over twelve days. I wanted to lie on my left or right side. I wanted to sit up and look around. I thought, *Well, it is almost over.*

Hopefully, I could sit up after the surgery and not have a fountain in my ear.

Chapter 25

Dangerous Surgery

I was so excited about getting the IV out of my neck, but I wasn't excited about them placing the needle in my left arm again. However, I knew the nurse had to do this. The nurse came in and said, "I'm here to place an IV in your arm and remove the one in your neck." I told her, "I have been expecting you." I showed her my arms and hands, and she said, "Oh, my, who did this? And why couldn't they find a vein in your arm?" I told her, "I was unconscious and I didn't know they were trying to put an IV in me. I have rolly veins, and everyone has trouble finding them." She told me, "If I don't get it in after two tries, I will stop." I agreed. First, she took the IV out of my neck and cleaned where it had been. *Good, that's over. But next is the dreaded IV in my arm.*

The nurse tried to get it in the first time, but the vein rolled away from the needle. Oh, that stung! I said, "One more time." After that, I said a prayer. She got it in the vein! Praise the Lord! Yes! It was finally over.

She looked at me and said, "You are absolutely correct. You do have rolly veins." I smiled at her and said, "At least it's over." Then she said, "Another nurse will be in here to get you ready for surgery." I thanked her again, and she left. I told my mom, "I wish we would have had her to do my veins in Knoxville. If we did, I would not be blue and black." We both laughed.

Brock and Faith had gone downstairs to get something to eat. Kent and Grant called that morning to tell me they were praying about my surgery. After that, my dad called me also. My mom was with me all the time. I have such a great family. Thank you, God. I wanted to tell my whole family, "I love you and thank you for everything."

The nurse came in. She put socks on my feet. The socks had happy faces on them. I guess she knew I *loved* happy faces. She told me, "Another nurse will shave a portion of hair on your right side." "Oh!" I exclaimed. "Well, I won't be going anywhere after I leave the hospital except for my house, so I won't worry about how my head or hair looks. I want my head to stop hurting and the surgery to be a success. Please!"

My children arrived before they took me to surgery. Everyone held hands and prayed. My mom prayed a beautiful prayer. When she finished, everyone hugged and kissed me. This was a wonderful feeling to have before I went into surgery.

Chapter 26

Dying or Waking Up

The nurses came in and told me, "It is time for surgery, but Dr. Wade is running thirty minutes late." I said, "That is fine. As long as he is here and is still going to operate on me today." They reassured me he was.

I gave my family a thumbs-up and then a big smile. I said, "It is time!" The nurses rolled me down a long hallway, and we went in an elevator. Next, we went down another long hallway and finally into the waiting room before surgery. They placed a warm gown on me and hooked me to several machines. After that, they started watching my vital signs. They also gave me morphine for my head pain. I started to relax.

(I found out two weeks after my surgery that Dr. Wade had gone back to my room before surgery started and talked to my mom. He told her, "Cheryl is very weak, and anything could happen in the surgery room. She has had spinal bacterial meningitis twice in fourteen months. That is enough for death. Plus, she also has the

CSF leakage." My mom told the doctor, "I will be praying for you and everyone else in the surgery room." He said, "Thanks," and then he left.)

My mom called her friends, and they started to pray that my brain would be in the correct spot and I would be strong enough to make it through surgery. While I was in the waiting room before my surgery, I could hear the nurses talking to each other about me. None of them had seen a CSF leakage as severe as mine. They also talked about me having spinal bacterial meningitis twice in fourteen months. They were surprised I was still alive. It was amazing to them. Two nurses were talking about me. By the end of their conversation, all of the nurses on the floor were standing around me. I hadn't had anything to eat or drink for fifteen hours and I was feeling dizzy. My head was in so much pain. One of the nurses looked at me and said, "You are very pale. Are you okay?" I told her, "My mouth is dry and I am getting sick." She said, "I am going to give you some medicine for the sickness." She gave me a shot. It helped some, but I was ready for the surgery to be over.

There was a clock on the wall in front of me, so I could see what time it was. Dr. Wade came to my bed. He smiled and patted my foot. He asked me, "Are you ready?" I said, "Yes, sir! Let's get this over with." He told the nurse to take off the cup on my ear. When she took it off, she gasped. She said, "Look at her ear. It looks like a small fountain. Watch the liquid come out." The cup was saturated when she removed it from my ear. I heard her ask the doctor, "How much liquid is she losing per minute?" The doctor told her. The nurses looked at each other and said, "How in the world is she alive while she is losing so much fluid?" The doctor looked at them and said, "I don't know." In a very low voice I heard that and thought, *God, God is the reason!* He had a purpose for me to live!

Dr. Wade told the nurse it was time. They pushed me to the operating room. The operating room was cooler than the room I had been in. I said a prayer. The nurse said, "I am going to give you something to relax you. The anesthesiologist will be in here shortly to put you to sleep." I said, "Okay." My main concern was whether I was going to wake up or not. I relaxed all right; the nurse put me to sleep.

Chapter 27

Surgery a Success or Not

What was that sound? I remember there was a tube down my throat, an oxygen device in my nose, and that sound again. Oh, it was the oxygen going into my nose. It felt awful. My throat was burning. I kept hearing, "Cheryl, Cheryl, the surgery is over. Can you wake up? Can you hear me?" I tried to talk, but my mouth felt like it had cotton in it. I tried to move and open my eyes, but it was like my body wouldn't work. I fell back to sleep.

The next time I woke up, I heard people talking. *Who are they and where am I?* I wondered. I couldn't remember where I was. I tried to open my eyes. Everything was blurry. I saw a clock on the wall, but I couldn't tell what time it was. I got scared. Was I dead? Then a lady came to me and said, "Cheryl, are you awake? The surgery is over." *Surgery,* I thought. *Oh, yes, now I remember. I am in Nashville having surgery on my ear and brain.*

I tried to talk, but still nothing came out. The nurses started asking me yes and no questions. I had to answer with a thumbs-up for yes and a thumbs-down for no. All I really wanted to know was if the surgery had been a success or not. After all their questions, they noticed my heartbeat was beating faster on the monitor. She asked me, "Are you scared and anxious?" I put both of my thumbs up! Yes! She said, "Dr. Wade will be in here soon to talk to you about what happened in surgery."

I lay there thinking and wondering if my CSF leakage was sealed. How was my brain? Would the surgery help me not to hear my heartbeat in my ear? My jaw and face were hurting tremendously. Before the surgery, I had told the nurse I had TMJ before and to please be careful with my jaw. She said she would write it on my chart. I could not open my jaw, and the right side of my face was numb. I kept thinking, *Did the surgery work? Please, someone tell me!* I fell back to sleep after that.

Chapter 28

Smiles :-)

I felt someone touch my foot. I opened my eyes and saw it was Dr. Wade. He was smiling. I thought, *I hope this is a good sign.* He started talking. "Cheryl, it went great! It was supposed to take me an hour and a half, but it took me around three and half hours. Your brain was full of infection. I don't know how you were living. This is the most infection I have ever seen in a brain. You had a CSF leakage for over three years. That is why you had headaches, neck aches, and stomachaches. Those caused you to be nauseated. The CSF leakage also caused you to get the spinal bacterial meningitis twice. I cleaned out your brain and ear. It was a mess. I haven't seen anything like it before. I repaired the CSF leakage and the bone that wasn't attached. Your brain was in the correct spot so I could lift it up, repair it, and clean it out. I cleaned out the spot where you had the CSF leakage. I gave you a new eardrum. I also repaired and cleaned out your ear. It had a large amount of scar tissue from all the other surgeries. You must have been in severe pain. It was awful when I opened up your ear to your brain. I cut the back of your ear from the top to the bottom. I put packing in your ear canal. Also, there is packing inside your ear, and it will dissolve in your body on its own. Your hearing should come back. I feel very confident about you getting your hearing back, but we will have to wait and see. I closed your Eustachian tube. You will not get spinal bacterial meningitis or the CSF leakage again."

I said, "Praise the Lord. God was behind you when you were operating on me." He smiled and said, "You can't get any of it wet for six weeks. Come back and see me in two weeks. I will remove the packing in your ear canal then. See you tomorrow."

I had so many questions to ask. My mouth opened, but no words came out. I waved good-bye and said with a sigh, "Thank you." The nurse told me later that the doctor went through my throat in the surgery to make sure everything was okay. He grafted skin from my ear to do the procedure. The nurses said, "The infection in your brain is something we will never forget."

Everyone in Knoxville and Nashville said I should have been dead. I am a miracle and a survivor because of God. Plus, I made it through the surgery, and they didn't think I would. I showed everyone that I could make it. I was extremely weak, but God helped me through all of the trauma and pain. All of the people who told me about the surgery had smiles on their faces. I started to smile. Let's just say I tried. It was a long but successful surgery. Praise the Lord!

They took all of my devices off except for the IV in my arm. They told me I had to stay on antibiotics for over a year to help my brain and ear. They took me back to my room. It was fantastic to see Brock, Faith, and my mom. My mom said she had called all of our family and told them the great news. Brock and Faith had texted everyone and told them the wonderful news. I didn't have a headache. No headache! That was a wonderful feeling. No fullness, no small pains, and no large pains in my head. I hadn't felt that good in almost four years. Thank you, Jesus! Together, we all prayed a thank-you prayer for my life.

I asked my mom, "Has Dr. Wade talked to you about the surgery?" She said, "Yes. He was on cloud nine when he finished your surgery. Everything went great."

It was quiet in the room. I said, "Mom, I don't have a headache, and I don't hear my heartbeat in my ear anymore." I was so happy. It felt great not having pressure in my head. The nurse came in and asked me if I was in any pain. I told her I could hardly move my jaw. I was in so much pain with it. They placed ice on my jaw and face. They gave me a shot of morphine. I had to live on a liquid diet again for two more weeks. I slept through most of the night because the drug that the anesthesiologist had given me was still in my body.

When I woke up, I was in severe pain from the top of my head to the bottom of my neck. *What is happening?* I thought. I opened my eyes and remembered where I was. I was in Nashville, Tennessee, and I had just had surgery. The nurses came in and checked my ear. Everything looked great. Dr. Wade came in and asked me, "How are you feeling today?" I was in so much pain, but that was what I expected from everything I had gone through in the past three weeks. "If everything keeps going good, you can go home tomorrow afternoon," Dr Wade said. I was so excited.

Chapter 29

Going Home

Thursday was a long and hard day. I had a hard time drinking liquid that day because my throat was so sore and my jaw wouldn't open. I didn't feel like sitting up or even walking. I just rested and took pain medicine all day. I never took pain medicine until the previous year when I had my first case of spinal bacterial meningitis.

On Thursday night, I couldn't sleep. The nurse had to give me a sleeping pill. This helped me get some sleep. I couldn't wait until the next day. I was finally going home. Praise the Lord! Friday was a happy day. I could finally put a straw in my mouth and drink water. The nurse came in and changed the bandage behind my ear. She said everything looked great.

Brock, Faith, and my mom packed our bags and put them in the car. They went to the hotel and packed what they had there. Then they checked out. I never got to see the hotel. I was there five days, and I never went out of the hospital.

Dr. Wade came in a little later that day to see me. He examined me and said, "Everything looks wonderful." I shook his hand and told him, "I feel like God has sent you to me." Then I thanked him. He signed my release forms.

The nurse told me all of my restrictions after surgery. She told me my next appointment was in three weeks because the next week was Thanksgiving and Dr. Wade wasn't going to be in his office. My mom helped me put on my clothes. Yes, no more hospital gowns! The nurse took the IV out of my arm. Three weeks of needles were gone, and it was needle-free time. I would finally get to take a warm shower. When I got home, I couldn't wash my hair but I could still run water on my body. I could laugh, but I still remember that every time the nurse came in the room, she would say, "Do you want a sponge bath?" I would feel sad. I just wanted a warm shower. I couldn't take a shower because they were afraid I would fall or get the IV wet.

Yes, finally! All the forms were filled out, and the wheelchair had just arrived. The nurse rolled me to my mom's car. Brock was driving us home. They had given me a morphine shot and a nausea shot for my ride home. I slept most of the way home with a smile on my face. I knew I would be home with my family soon. I couldn't wait.

Chapter 30

My Wonderful Home and Family

We arrived home later that evening in darkness. I couldn't see very well, but I knew I was home when Brock pulled in our driveway. *I am home,* I thought. *Praise the Lord!* Three weeks had been an extremely long time to be away. My kids came to greet me, and I was so glad to see them. I couldn't bend down for another four weeks, so I just talked to my animals without petting them.

Faith helped me inside. The smell of my home was refreshing! My sons Kent and Grant came and hugged me. My dad was there too. It was great being all together again with my family again. It had been a tough time, but our family had come closer together and learned how to depend on each other. We all came together and prayed a thank-you prayer. We thanked God for every miracle and for letting me come home.

I had to go to different doctors in Knoxville once a week for a checkup. My energy level was extremely low, but in time it will get better. I only stayed on pain pills a week and a half. I have no hearing in my right ear. Dr. Wade said it will take time. There is still packing inside my head, and it will dissolve in time. I have no feeling around my right ear, but the doctor said it would take one year to come back. He told me in one year I should be like new. Praise the Lord!

I am so glad I didn't stay in a coma or a no-response state. I'm happy that God brought me out of that. I'm excited that God has a purpose for me. I'm glad my family kept talking to me. That's the reason I woke up and decided I didn't want to die. I still have work to do on earth for God and my family. Life is precious. Don't take anything for granted. Cherish each moment of life. Be thankful each day for everything God has done for you. Life is fantastic with God in it. Smile. God loves you. All of these thoughts were going through my mind.

I have missed out on a lot of events since I have been sick. I have missed family gatherings, going out to eat, work, events at work, my sons' baseball and basketball games, the musical my daughter participated in, judgment house (we had not missed it for eleven years), walking with my dog, and being out in public, and I could go on. But I'm thankful to be alive. My disease specialist, Dr. Terry, was very cautious with my health this time. She had me stay away from all sicknesses by making me remain isolated in my house for three months. God saved me three times in fourteen months. My life is exceptional.

Conclusion

I felt that God wanted me to write this book and share my testimony with different churches and people all over the world. I'm so excited about my goal. God is wonderful, and I want to share that with the world. He gave me strength and courage to fight for my life. This experience has taught me that life is precious and that everyone should thank God for everything every day.

Remember that your life can change in one minute!

CPSIA information can be obtained at www.ICGtesting.com
Printed in the USA
LVOW041033100312

272433LV00002B/2/P